DOOMSCROLLING ↓
LED↓
TO ↓
DOOM.

TYLER LAZARUS
STUMP
AKA MISTER.E

ISBN
Fonts by Jess Latham. Thank You.
Printed, Distributed and Bound in the United States of America First Printing
SEPTEMBER 2024
Published by He Who Rebels Against All
Oklahoma City, Oklahoma 73106

Hey, Thanks for getting a copy!
IF you like these, check out my other works
XOXO

Big Government Always Equals Big TROUBLE.

"it won't be like that." the 19 times vaccinated, recent heart attack patient says, with 5 genders, and a "I LOVE THE CDC" bracelet. And a ukraine tattoo on their left ass. Also, overweight.

It will. It was. It will be.
It will never be good.

Put small minds in charge OF critical agencies,
and you have endorsed big corruption.

Allow small amounts of critical thinking,
and you enable big amounts of ignorance
(that thinks itself truly wise)

"Well, Trump…."

TRUMP NOTHING.
BIDEN NOTHING.
☞☜☛☚☺☹

WORSHIP OF THESE TWO DUMB FUCKS
HAS TRUMPED ALL REASON,
INCLUDING: COMMON GROUND AND COMMON SENSE.

SHUT.

THEE.

FUCK.
UP. ☝

The nuance of allowing government agencies to run amok isn't
about any specific figurehead,
it's about how an inability to question leadership
leaves a country with the BLIND leading THE BLIND.

Don't you see?

This is about what happens when fools assume power,
are allowed unlimited amounts of it,
catapulted up into positions they don't deserve, are totally
unequipped for, and incapable of navigating the complex
world of political science....

and the little people who voted for (THOSE IDIOTS)
end up

SUFFERING.

BECAUSE. OF. IT.

TERRIBLE POLICY
ENDS IN
TERRIBLE CONSEQUENCE.

DOOMSCROLLING... LED TO DOOM

BY TYLER LAZARUS STUMP
AKA MISTER. E

CHAPTER 1
After watching chaos and pandaemonium
unleash themselves across the American/
Americana landscape, I vanished back to the

shadows.

Fauci got away with murder,
the American Gov-uh-ment got away with high
treason, China watched it all, ate their fried rice
and eggrolls and probably/honestly laughed….
and Americans were left high and dry,
or really, triple vaccinated and dying.

I moved back to the shadows,
and became a shadowy figure,
because there was nothing I could do.

I can't rip those mRNA products out of body
systems. I can't drain that poison from
cardiovascular tissue.

Cardiomyopathy and Cardiac arrest became
normalized,
when people (the guv-uh-ment and co)
should have been the ONES arrested.

But who do you call when the Good guys are now
THE BAD GUYS.
twirls pigtails, phones the police *chews gum*

911, um, my own government just committed state sponsored terrorism on its own populace and killed 1 million americans. Yeah. Help. Send a deputy.

> ??????????????

I can't defer to authority because THEY are THE AUTHORITY.

So, again,
back to the shadows,

and more importantly….

Back to the Drawing Board.

Intermission: ELON MUSK (ROCKET MAN) ACQUIRES TWITTER, CHANGES THE NAME to 'X.'
AND WHILE THE BIRD MAY BE GONE,
THE LEFTIST BIRDBRAINS STILL LINGER ON.

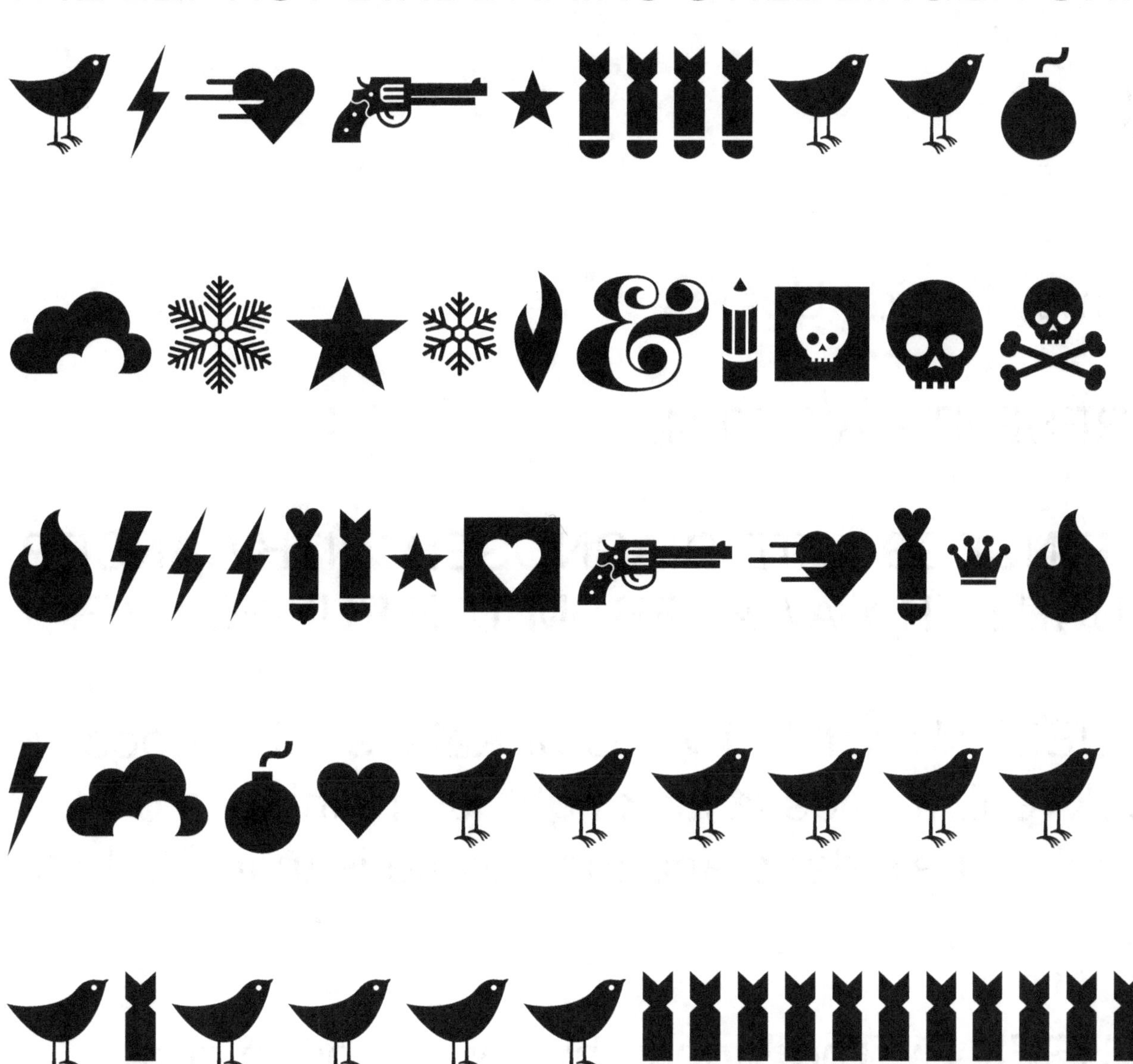

Time Speeds Up

PRESENT DAY: 2024.

"PRINCESS KATE DIAGNOSED WITH CANCER. CURRENTLY AWAY FROM THE PUBLIC EYE."

X USER: "I bet that video of Kate is A.I. It doesn't look real. It doesn't look right, something is off. Maybe she's dead and the palace is trying to hide it…"

X USER 2: "The Monarchy always been corrupt, wouldn't surprise me if they're trying to buy themselves a bit of time. Poor dear is probably already dead."

 ☠

JOURNAL OF ONCOLOGY: DOCTORS ARE BAFFLED BY THE SUDDEN AND DRAMATIC RISE IN CANCERS IN YOUNG

ADULTS.

X USER: My niece developed stage 4 cancer after her third Pfizer.

X USER 2: Same, sudden breast cancer in my mother after her booster…

X USER 3: Will any of these people be held accountable for doing this crime against humanity?

X USER 4: PUSSY IN BIO, CLICK FOR ONLY FANS.

THE ARIES ECLIPSE BRINGS A NEW
SENSE OF PURPOSE IN YOUR LIFE
FIXED SIGNS WILL EXPERIENCE THE
CHANGE THE MOST.

*

BIRD FLU SPREADING ACROSS FARMS
IN AMERICA, HOW DANGEROUS IS THIS
STRAND OF H5N1

*

X USER: HEY BRO, DO YOU LIKE MY
DICK?

*

TRENDING: AQUARIUS, AZEALIA BANKS,
THE WEF, THE WEEKEND

while in the last (almost) 5 years,
these people have done stupid things,
they aren't totally stupid.

everyone knows and realizes america is falling apart and
things are turning to shit,

they know it's happening.

but they can't get off their phones to actually do anything
about it.

they are glued to their devices.
these devices with fancy screens which will be their undoing.

if they don't start to do something about all of it.

that's the point of the book.

doomscrolling through social media insanity is causing the
doom of this republic and the death of our democracy.

reading about corruption is one thing.

fixing it... is another.

entirely.

but that isn't the entire problem,

most can see and most know how wrong
things are becoming,

but the way the power structure works,
they feel powerless to do anything.

but they aren't powerless.

but it does require willpower to oppose
this kind of corruption.

you have to do something.

not just in words,
but deeds.

⇓ ↓

the problem of it all is, it's simply much easier to sit on your phone and scroll as the world worsens, then actually doing anything to fix that world, because the problems of the world, even when they interfere directly with us, seem bigger than us, and somehow removed from us...

when they are immediately impacting us.

They are right here.
<ins>and now.</ins>
↓

⇨ They are ruining the quality of our lives. lmao.

They aren't far off or far way.

↓

But at this moment, let me say this.

Because, before I wrote this next line, I was MIA (reading the other books I've written for this series, because they all connect) and deciding how I want to phrase this,
in the totality of all my other works.

Here is the deal.

and here, equally, is the problem.

if you remember nothing else from any of my other books, because you A. have dementia, or B. you're retarded, do remember this...

The reason things are falling apart isn't because people can't unite and fix them,

it's because.

The attention span of the average person is being skewed in 100 different directions, in any given day, everyday.

The focus to fix these problems is known,
but these people can't focus long enough to do it.

That's the problem.

NOBODY WITH SENSE
wants to live inside a dysfunctional system
that negatively hurts them or diminishes the
quality of their life.

but... when intentional distractions and
synthetic chaos are created in order to move
their attention to "another problem," they cant
fix the first five before it, because their mind
is already onto the latest/newest/most
outrageous fire.

and this is by design.

because... as all this horeshit keeps
happening on a global level, people keep
scrolling through each mini-event, passively
watching and not able to fix or solve the root
issues underlying it, because by the time they
gather up the will, the fortitude and the
needed volition,

SOMETHING ELSE
has happened.

here is the biggest issue of dem' all, dawh-lingz.

nobody is reading books anymore.

they are now on their phones.

like, right now, right this moment,

right dis second.

peoples are scrolling through their devices, reading junk, listening to crap, and absorbing mindless gunk,entertainment,escapism content on durr phones.

Books are a cultural relic of 40 years ago.

Honestly, maybe even more.

Yea, some still read.

but the world ... is on the world wide web.

That's where the activity is happeninnnnnnnnn.

I would honestly even argue - and I would be correct - that not even the mainstream, legacy media is cultivating the attention... like they once did.

MSN,NBC,ABC. DEFG, ... all these networks really have fallen because of social networks.

Again, yea, they have some viewers,
but not LIKE they did.

Because the hive and the human hivemind is all online.

And not this line, or an old fashioned phone line can call any of it out.

Because there no longer is anyone THERE to pick up the damn phone.

Their phone is being utilized to scroll through the world on fire.

And they won't listen, even if you could reach them with the truth of this message.

DOOMSCROLL

ING

LED ⇓

TO ➤➤➤➤

DOOM. ↵